escapes

TAKE A MOMENT TO
CONNECT TO YOURSELF

Written by: M.H. Clark

Designed & Illustrated by: Sarah Forster

TAKE A MOMENT
TO LOOK INWARD.

———

If you could choose a feeling to

carry with you today, what would

it be? Calmness, enthusiasm,

groundedness, excitement, peace?

These pages are full of guided meditations to connect you to yourself.

Get comfortable. Pick the destination that's right for this moment, and read it—silently, or aloud. What do you notice?

Some part of you will come alive in this place. Some part of you will ask to be seen. Some part of you will change on this journey.

You'll find something to take with you, something to keep, something to return to again and again.

TAKE A MOMENT TO
CONNECT TO YOURSELF.

take this moment
to begin.

DESERT

Out in the desert, night is coming on. The setting

sun paints the sky orange and purple and gold,

and one by one, uncountable numbers of stars

appear. The air is warm and heavy around you, and

smells of dust and campfire and sage. The ground

holds on to the day, and the rocks still radiate heat

from the sun. Take off your shoes and stand on

the earth. In this moment, how do you feel?

ROCKY COAST

———

Here, where the water meets the land, the granite rocks are grey and black and green, and sparkle in the sun. There are small tide pools where the waves splash over, and inside each one is a tiny, vibrant world—little shells and seaweed and stones. You stand facing the sea and watch the waves crash into white foam, hitting against the land and washing back. You close your eyes.

In this moment, how do you feel?

SNOWY CEDAR FOREST

After the snowfall, even the quiet is quieter here,

and the world feels very far away. The tops of

the cedar trees, so high above, make this place a

sanctuary—just these ancient trees and their deep

stillness and their blanket of white. You choose

a tree to stand in front of, and see the way the

snow has settled into the bark where the wind

has blown it. Place your hands on its trunk.

In this moment, how do you feel?

THERE IS ROOM HERE
FOR YOU TO BE YOURSELF.

everything
you are.

MEADOW WITH FLOWERS

Halfway up the mountain, the sunlit meadow is radiant with wildflowers—a sea of purple, white, and blue. The air is gentle, the sky is clear, the snowcapped peak in the distance is huge and calm and reassuring. Everything around it seems so small. Take a moment to rest after the hike, to feel the breath in your lungs and the sun on your face. Stand tall and strong and capable right here, where you are. In this moment, how do you feel?

TRAVEL MORNING

———

You wake to the sound of the bell tower, and
the birds on the roof, and voices in the street
below. Opening the shutters, you are here—your
first day in this new place—this ancient city,
the cobblestone streets, the narrow alley where
bright laundry flutters in the wind. The smell of
coffee wafts up from a little street café below.
The whole day awaits you, in this new place.
In this moment, how do you feel?

LUSH RAINFOREST

———

Have you ever seen so many shades of green?
Look up at the leaves of all these different trees,
the delicate mosses on their bark, the tangled
vines—you are surrounded by life. You hear the
chattering of birds, high up in the canopy, where
the sunlight filters through in gentle rays. And
somewhere close is a waterfall—its rushing sound
clears your mind. Stand here; notice yourself.
In this moment, how do you feel?

THERE IS A PART OF YOU THAT
REMAINS CALM AND UNCHANGING.

*breathe in
and find it.*

WHITE SAND BEACH

———

The sand beneath your feet is white—crisp and

bright and sparkling white—and the sun is high

overhead. The turquoise waters are so calm—just

gentle little waves, and a single sailboat, far out

in the bay. You listen. The only sound is the *shhh*

of those waves and the sea wind rustling the

tops of the palm trees. Just a whisper. Feel

the gentle heat from the sand on your feet

and the warmth of the sun on your skin.

In this moment, how do you feel?

CHERRY BLOSSOMS

The footbridge arches over a little stream,

and the path beyond it leads to the garden.

The cherry trees are in full bloom—pink blossoms

on the dark branches, pink blossoms on the path,

even petals blowing in the wind. The light here

is like an embrace, gentle and profound, and

everything it touches is blush colored and

beautiful. You take a moment to stand here,

to bask in this beauty, to take in this air.

In this moment, how do you feel?

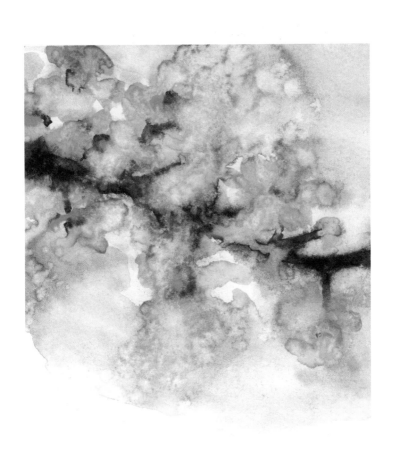

NORTHERN LIGHTS

You stand in the winter night, looking up, where the northern lights draw curtains of color across the sky. They are pale green, magenta, and luminous red, shimmering against the dark sky, and illuminating the ragged silhouettes of the far-off pines. The lights fade and shift and reappear, changing endlessly, almost alive above you. Breathe out, and watch the white cloud of your breath in front of you.

In this moment, how do you feel?

WHAT IS YOUR HEART
ASKING FOR? WHAT IS IT

drawing you
towards?

FARMERS' MARKET

It is early morning, but the vendors have already set up their stalls in the old stone square. The morning air is still cool, and smells of bread and spice and citrus peel. You walk through the aisles of the market, taking it all in—the stacks of bright fruit, the woven baskets, bins of olives, golden pastries. Everything calls to you at once, but you stop at a stall selling glasses of tea, and buy one to sip on and warm your hands.

In this moment, how do you feel?

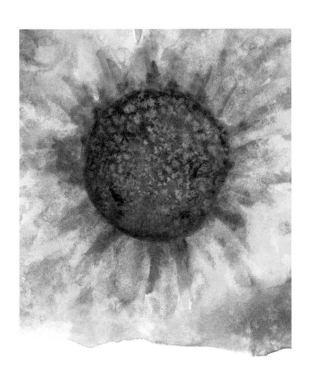

FALL LEAVES

———

Take a breath. The air around you is crisp and clean. Above you and everywhere, as far as you can see, the hills are a brilliant show of maple leaves—orange and rust and fiery red. With the sun shining through, each leaf is jewel-like and astonishing, in perfect contrast against the clear blue sky. A single hawk circles, high above on a current of air, and coasts down to the valley below. In this moment, how do you feel?

LAKE SUNSET

———

Evenings here are so calm. Walk out to the end of the worn wooden dock and sit down. Let your feet dangle. The boats rock gently where they are moored, and you listen to the water as it laps against their hulls. Late summer has its hold on things, warm and heavy and slow. Far off, across the lake, a cabin is lit—just one warm and welcoming light. The colors of the sky are deepening, and the water changes too.

In this moment, how do you feel?

what do you notice in this moment?

WHAT WOULD YOU LIKE TO CHANGE?
AND WHAT WOULD YOU LIKE TO KEEP?

ART MUSEUM

———

Through the tall glass doors, the galleries are
silent. The light on each painting is focused and
gentle, and brings the work to life—these paintings
with colors like sunsets and colors like water.
You sit on a bench and allow yourself to let the
world fall away. You allow yourself to look at this
painting until you notice how the colors fold into
each other, and where the brushstrokes meet—
until this painting feels like its own small world.
In this moment, how do you feel?

RUSHING RIVER

———

The water rushing by you now is spring's first

snowmelt, from the top of the mountain. Standing

here, on the pebbled shore, you can feel how cold

it is, and how powerful. You watch the shifting

currents, how they carry leaves and branches on

their way. And you listen to these waters, and the

story they are telling, as they roll over rocks and

make small white waves and whirlpools.

In this moment, how do you feel?

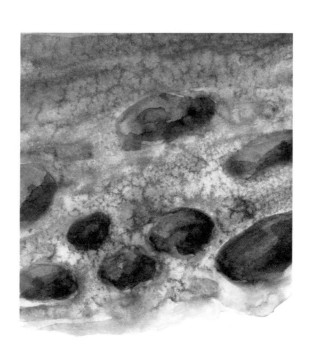

FIELD OF GRASSES

The late light across the fields is golden, and
the grass is golden, too. Out here, everything is
so flat that the sky seems bigger, bluer, closer.
The landscape almost holds you here—this
huge sky, and the tall grass billowing, shifting,
moving like waves on the sea. You watch the sun
change the far-off hills, shifting gold and green.
You watch the swallows dipping and weaving
high and then low, flying for the joy of it.
In this moment, how do you feel?

CITY LIGHTS

From this high window, the lights of the city spread out like stars. You see the way they map the streets, the buildings, the lives so many people lead. There are lights for people reading, lights for people working, lights to welcome people home. And far off, lights on bridges spanning the river, shining on each arch and pillar. From your quiet room, you imagine a light for each person in this city—every single life. In this moment, how do you feel?

WHAT DO YOU WANT TO
BRING WITH YOU TODAY?

how do you want
this day to be?